GOD'S GRACE

for

—

GRADUATES

B&H
PUBLISHING GROUP

NASHVILLE, TENNESSEE

CONTENTS

INTRODUCTION

Life tends to maneuver us into categories, into penciled-in bubbles on the random identification form. Some of them we like; some we don't. Some we actively seek out and continue to pursue; some were sitting there waiting for us and won't turn us loose.

But one thing we all know: deep inside these simple boxes and check marks reside entire worlds crawling with complication, challenge, and difficulty. Even if easy to get into, they are rarely so easy to faithfully, successfully, and steadily keep going through.

As a new graduate, for instance, you may often feel inadequate to the task ahead of you. Your days are likely full of activity yet can still feel unfinished. You try maximizing the jobs your particular box (or boxes) entails, yet they maddeningly resist being colored all the way to the edges. You're closing one chapter, and starting a whole new one.

The reason this book exists is because God's grace never met a check box it couldn't fill with hope, peace, direction, and perspective—with motivation, counsel, freedom, and opportunity. This book is here, and is now yours, because the Bible not only speaks timelessly to everyone but specifically to you . . . with grace. God's grace. Sufficient to every place. Even to the places you're living this very moment.

ACCEPTANCE

If God is for us, who can be against us? Our eternal reassurance in the face of conflicts, rejection, or uncertainty is that God's love for us is constant.

ᕷ

But the LORD said to Samuel, "Do not look at his appearance or his stature because I have rejected him. Humans do not see what the Lord sees, for humans see what is visible, but the LORD sees the heart."
    1 Samuel 16:7

ᕷ

"Everyone the Father gives me will come to me, and the one who comes to me I will never cast out."
    John 6:37

ᕷ

But God proves his own love for us in that while we were still sinners, Christ died for us.
    Romans 5:8

If God is for us, who is against us?
Romans 8:31

Peter began to speak: "Now I truly understand that God doesn't show favoritism, but in every nation the person who fears him and does what is right is acceptable to him."
Acts 10:34–35

Heavenly Father, thank You that no matter what hardships I might face, You have accepted me as Your Son and You have a plan for my future.

ANGER

Anger is an emotion that can reveal to us our values. The key, however, is not to act out in anger but to speak and act with love.

∽

Refrain from anger and give up your rage;
do not be agitated—it can only bring harm.
        Psalm 37:8

∽

A patient person shows great understanding,
but a quick-tempered one promotes foolishness.
        Proverbs 14:29

∽

A gentle answer turns away anger,
but a harsh word stirs up wrath.
        Proverbs 15:1

"But I tell you, everyone who is angry with his brother or sister will be subject to judgment. Whoever insults his brother or sister, will be subject to the court. Whoever says, 'You fool!' will be subject to hellfire."
Matthew 5:22

Be angry and do not sin. Don't let the sun go down on your anger, and don't give the devil an opportunity.
Ephesians 4:26–27

Lord, may Your Holy Spirit guide my words
and actions when I'm feeling angry so that
I can show grace to those around me.

ANXIETY

Lurking beneath all our anxieties is the desire to be in control—but we will find peace when we remember that the Creator of the cosmos has us safely in His hands.

"Therefore I tell you: Don't worry about your life, what you will eat or what you will drink; or about your body, what you will wear. Isn't life more than food and the body more than clothing? Consider the birds of the sky: They don't sow or reap or gather into barns, yet your heavenly Father feeds them. Aren't you worth more than they? Can any of you add one moment to his life-span by worrying?"
      Matthew 6:25–27

"Peace I leave with you. My peace I give to you. I do not give to you as the world gives. Don't let your heart be troubled or fearful."
      John 14:27

Don't worry about anything, but in everything, through prayer and petition with thanksgiving, present your requests to God. And the peace of God, which surpasses all understanding, will guard your hearts and minds in Christ Jesus.
Philippians 4:6–7

For God has not given us a spirit of fear, but one of power, love, and sound judgment.
2 Timothy 1:7

Humble yourselves, therefore, under the mighty hand of God, so that he may exalt you at the proper time, casting all your cares on him, because he cares about you.
1 Peter 5:6–7

Dear God, I entrust to You all the bills, decisions, relationships, and situations that feel so out of my control, knowing that Your peace will guard my heart and mind.

AUTHORITY

As you make your way into adult life, you will encounter all sorts of human authorities, but ultimately God is in control of every sphere of life.

∞

Then he said to them, "Give, then, to Caesar the things that are Caesar's, and to God the things that are God's." When they heard this, they were amazed. So they left him and went away.
   Matthew 22:21–22

∞

Jesus came near and said to them, "All authority has been given to me in heaven and on earth."
   Matthew 28:18

∞

Let everyone submit to the governing authorities, since there is no authority except from God, and the authorities that exist are instituted by God.
   Romans 13:1

For this reason God highly exalted him
and gave him the name
that is above every name,
so that at the name of Jesus
every knee will bow—
in heaven and on earth
and under the earth—
and every tongue will confess
that Jesus Christ is Lord,
to the glory of God the Father.
  Philippians 2:9–11

Submit to every human authority because of the Lord, whether to the
emperor as the supreme authority or to governors as those sent out
by him to punish those who do what is evil and to praise those who do
what is good. For it is God's will that you silence the ignorance of foolish
people by doing good.
  1 Peter 2:13–15

Lord, please grant me wisdom so that I
may be humble and respectful in my interactions
with those in positions of authority.

CHANGE

Graduating from school can be both an exciting and scary time of life—but in all seasons and phases, the presence of God goes with you.

There is an occasion for everything,
and a time for every activity under heaven.
    Ecclesiastes 3:1

"Do not remember the past events, pay no attention to things of old.
Look, I am about to do something new; even now it is coming. Do you not
see it? Indeed, I will make a way in the wilderness, rivers in the desert."
    Isaiah 43:18–19

"Because I, the LORD, have not changed, you descendants of Jacob have
not been destroyed."
    Malachi 3:6

Therefore, if anyone is in Christ, he is a new creation; the old has passed away, and see, the new has come!
    2 Corinthians 5:17

❧

Jesus Christ is the same yesterday, today, and forever.
    Hebrews 13:8

❧

Lord Jesus, no matter what the future brings, may I take heart that You are with me until the end of the age.

COMPASSION

God calls Christians to love our neighbors as ourselves and to love our enemies despite what they may have done—true compassion is acting out of love in the best interests of others.

Yet he was compassionate;
he atoned for their iniquity
and did not destroy them.
He often turned his anger aside
and did not unleash all his wrath.
Psalm 78:38

When he went ashore, he saw a large crowd and had compassion on them, because they were like sheep without a shepherd. Then he began to teach them many things.
Mark 6:34

Carry one another's burdens; in this way you will fulfill the law of Christ.
Galatians 6:2

∽

And be kind and compassionate to one another, forgiving one another, just as God also forgave you in Christ.
Ephesians 4:32

∽

Dear God, may Your Holy Spirit fill my heart and soul with concern for others so I may be a willing conduit of your love.

CONFIDENCE

Remember that, no matter what challenges you may face, the power that created the universe and raised Christ from the dead lives inside of you.

Do not fear, for I am with you; do not be afraid, for I am your God. I will strengthen you; I will help you; I will hold on to you with my righteous right hand.
    Isaiah 41:10

It is not that we are competent in ourselves to claim anything as coming from ourselves, but our adequacy is from God.
    2 Corinthians 3:5

I am able to do all things through him who strengthens me.
    Philippians 4:13

So don't throw away your confidence, which has a great reward. For you need endurance, so that after you have done God's will, you may receive what was promised.

    Hebrews 10:35–36

∽

This is how we will know that we belong to the truth and will reassure our hearts before him whenever our hearts condemn us; for God is greater than our hearts, and he knows all things. Dear friends, if our hearts don't condemn us, we have confidence before God and receive whatever we ask from him because we keep his commands and do what is pleasing in his sight.

    1 John 3:19–22

∽

Heavenly Father, grant me the kind of inner strength and confidence that only comes from trusting in Your love and provision for all my needs.

CONTENTMENT

The quickest route to contentment is through gratitude and trust—recognize the abundant goodness in your life and trust that God never fails to provide for your needs.

"So don't worry, saying, 'What will we eat?' or 'What will we drink?' or 'What will we wear?' For the Gentiles eagerly seek all these things, and your heavenly Father knows that you need them. But seek first the kingdom of God and his righteousness, and all these things will be provided for you. Therefore don't worry about tomorrow, because tomorrow will worry about itself. Each day has enough trouble of its own."
Matthew 6:31–34

He then told them, "Watch out and be on guard against all greed, because one's life is not in the abundance of his possessions."
Luke 12:15

I don't say this out of need, for I have learned to be content in whatever circumstances I find myself. I know both how to make do with little, and I know how to make do with a lot. In any and all circumstances I have learned the secret of being content—whether well fed or hungry, whether in abundance or in need.

Philippians 4:11–12

But godliness with contentment is great gain. For we brought nothing into the world, and we can take nothing out. If we have food and clothing, we will be content with these.

1 Timothy 6:6–8

Keep your life free from the love of money. Be satisfied with what you have, for he himself has said, I will never leave you or abandon you.

Hebrews 13:5

Heavenly Father, thank You for Your unfailing love and faithfulness and may You grow in me a godly contentment.

COURAGE

Having courage doesn't mean that you feel no fear; rather it means having a willingness and readiness to proceed despite the fear.

Haven't I commanded you: be strong and courageous? Do not be afraid or discouraged, for the LORD your God is with you wherever you go."
    Joshua 1:9

I always let the LORD guide me.
Because he is at my right hand,
I will not be shaken.
    Psalm 16:8

Wait for the LORD;
be strong, and let your heart be courageous.
Wait for the LORD.
    Psalm 27:14

Be alert, stand firm in the faith, be courageous, be strong.
  1 Corinthians 16:13

✑

For God has not given us a spirit of fear, but one of power, love, and sound judgment.
  2 Timothy 1:7

✑

Dear God, grant me a sense of Your strength and presence that I may face this day and its challenges with courage.

CREATIVITY

Being made in the image of God means that every person is also endowed with the creativity of the Creator.

So God created man in his own image; he created him in the image of God; he created them male and female.
> Genesis 1:27

I will praise you
because I have been remarkably and wondrously made.
Your works are wondrous,
and I know this very well.
> Psalm 139:14

So God created man in his own image; he created him in the image of God; he created them male and female.
> Genesis 1:27

Do you see a person skilled in his work? He will stand in the presence of kings. He will not stand in the presence of the unknown.
> Proverbs 22:29

All things were created through him, and apart from him not one thing was created that has been created.

 John 1:3

For we are his workmanship, created in Christ Jesus for good works, which God prepared ahead of time for us to do.

 Ephesians 2:10

Lord Jesus, through whom all things were made, guide my mind, heart, and hands to create goodness and beauty in every aspect of my daily life.

DECEPTION

Throughout any given week, we may be tempted to deceive others—blatant lies, omission of truth, subtle falsehoods—but our calling is to be people of integrity.

∽

The one who lives with integrity lives securely,
but whoever perverts his ways will be found out.
    Proverbs 10:9

∽

Lying lips are detestable to the LORD,
but faithful people are his delight.
    Proverbs 12:22

∽

"You are of your father the devil, and you want to carry out your
father's desires. He was a murderer from the beginning and does not
stand in the truth, because there is no truth in him. When he tells a lie, he
speaks from his own nature, because he is a liar and the father of lies."
    John 8:44

Dear friends, do not believe every spirit, but test the spirits to see if they are from God, because many false prophets have gone out into the world.

1 John 4:1

∽

Dear God, may Your Spirit within empower me to be truthful and loving in all of my encounters with others in my life.

DEPRESSION

In your darkest hours, hold fast to the truth that God is the God of all comfort, who comforts us in all our affliction so that we may be able to comfort others.

⟡

The LORD sits enthroned over the flood;
the LORD sits enthroned, King forever.
The LORD gives his people strength;
the LORD blesses his people with peace.
        Psalm 29:10–11

⟡

Answer me quickly, LORD;
my spirit fails.
Don't hide your face from me,
or I will be like those going down to the Pit.
Let me experience
your faithful love in the morning,
for I trust in you.
Reveal to me the way I should go
because I appeal to you.
        Psalm 143:7–8

The LORD is near the brokenhearted;
he saves those crushed in spirit.
  Psalm 34:18

Do not fear, for I am with you; do not be afraid, for I am your God. I will
strengthen you; I will help you; I will hold on to you with my righteous
right hand.
  Isaiah 41:10

I will give you the treasures of darkness and riches from secret places, so
that you may know that I am the LORD. I am the God of Israel, who calls
you by your name.
  Isaiah 45:3

Lord Jesus, You were a man of sorrows, acquainted
with grief. Pour out Your love and strength on my
aching heart and bring me Your grace and comfort.

DISCERNMENT

The Holy Spirit is our ever-present Helper who grants us wisdom so we can know and do the will of God.

So give your servant a receptive heart to judge your people and to discern between good and evil. For who is able to judge this great people of yours?
    1 Kings 3:9

And I pray this: that your love will keep on growing in knowledge and every kind of discernment, so that you may approve the things that are superior and may be pure and blameless in the day of Christ.
    Philippians 1:9–10

Don't stifle the Spirit. Don't despise prophecies, but test all things. Hold on to what is good. Stay away from every kind of evil.
    1 Thessalonians 5:19–22

Now if any of you lacks wisdom, he should ask God—who gives to all generously and ungrudgingly—and it will be given to him.
  James 1:5

Dear friends, do not believe every spirit, but test the spirits to see if they are from God, because many false prophets have gone out into the world.
  1 John 4:1

Holy Spirit, may my spirit be open and receptive to Your prompting and leading so that I discern what is right and good.

DISCIPLINE

As a young adult making your way in the world, an essential path of growth is cultivating self-discipline: do the right thing at the right time in the right way.

❧

Whoever loves discipline loves knowledge,
but one who hates correction is stupid.
    Proverbs 12:1

❧

The one who will not use the rod hates his son,
but the one who loves him disciplines him diligently.
    Proverbs 13:24

❧

Foolishness is bound to the heart of a youth;
a rod of discipline will separate it from him.
    Proverbs 22:15

Instead, I discipline my body and bring it under strict control, so that after preaching to others, I myself will not be disqualified.
    1 Corinthians 9:27

No discipline seems enjoyable at the time, but painful. Later on, however, it yields the peaceful fruit of righteousness to those who have been trained by it.
    Hebrews 12:11

Heavenly Father, may Your hand guide me and correct me so that all I do and say will glorify You.

DISCOURAGEMENT

When our hopes are dashed or we fail in an endeavor, we can remember that the God of hope will fill us with joy, peace, and strength.

The LORD is the one who will go before you. He will be with you; he will not leave you or abandon you. Do not be afraid or discouraged.
    Deuteronomy 31:8

I have told you these things so that in me you may have peace. You will have suffering in this world. Be courageous! I have conquered the world.
    John 16:33

Now may the God of hope fill you with all joy and peace as you believe so that you may overflow with hope by the power of the Holy Spirit.
    Romans 15:13

In the same way the Spirit also helps us in our weakness, because we do not know what to pray for as we should, but the Spirit himself intercedes for us with unspoken groanings. And he who searches our hearts knows the mind of the Spirit, because he intercedes for the saints according to the will of God. We know that all things work together for the good of those who love God, who are called according to his purpose.

Romans 8:26–28

But he said to me, "My grace is sufficient for you, for my power is perfected in weakness."
Therefore, I will most gladly boast all the more about my weaknesses, so that Christ's power may reside in me.

2 Corinthians 12:9

Lord, sometimes it's hard to remember that You're in control of everything. Please grant me Your grace and strength in this moment of discouragement.

DISSATISFIED

When we feel dissatisfied with our lives or circumstances, we can rediscover the abundance around us by practicing gratitude and thanksgiving.

∽

For he has satisfied the thirsty
and filled the hungry with good things.
    Psalm 107:9

∽

You open your hand
and satisfy the desire of every living thing.
    Psalm 145:16

∽

"I am the bread of life," Jesus told them. "No one who comes to me
will ever be hungry, and no one who believes in me will ever be thirsty
again."
    John 6:35

The LORD will always lead you,
satisfy you in a parched land,
and strengthen your bones.
You will be like a watered garden
and like a spring whose water never runs dry.
Isaiah 58:11

Now may the God of hope fill you with all joy and peace as you believe
so that you may overflow with hope by the power of the Holy Spirit.
Romans 15:13

Dear God, no good thing do You withhold from Your
people. Help me see the goodness all around me and
to delight in Your good and perfect gifts.

DRUNKENNESS

Whether you're seeking to relieve stress or enjoy time with friends, take care to make choices that are godly and healthy.

∽

"Be on your guard, so that your minds are not dulled from carousing, drunkenness, and worries of life, or that day will come on you unexpectedly like a trap. For it will come on all who live on the face of the whole earth. But be alert at all times, praying that you may have strength to escape all these things that are going to take place and to stand before the Son of Man."
    Luke 21:34–38

∽

For the grace of God has appeared, bringing salvation for all people, instructing us to deny godlessness and worldly lusts and to live in a sensible, righteous, and godly way in the present age, while we wait for the blessed hope, the appearing of the glory of our great God and Savior, Jesus Christ.
    Titus 2:11–13

Let us walk with decency, as in the daytime: not in carousing and drunkenness; not in sexual impurity and promiscuity; not in quarreling and jealousy.

Romans 13:13

✍

Wine is a mocker, beer is a brawler;
whoever goes astray because of them is not wise.

Proverbs 20:1

✍

So don't be foolish, but understand what the Lord's will is. And don't get drunk with wine, which leads to reckless living, but be filled by the Spirit: speaking to one another in psalms, hymns, and spiritual songs, singing and making music with your heart to the Lord, giving thanks always for everything to God the Father in the name of our Lord Jesus Christ, submitting to one another in the fear of Christ.

Ephesians 5:17–21

✍

Lord God, may my heart and soul overflow
with the joy of knowing You, and let this joy
be my strength in moments of weakness.

FAILURE

Though failures of any kind can crush our spirits, we have the assurance that God's plans never fail.

Now we have this treasure in clay jars, so that this extraordinary power may be from God and not from us. We are afflicted in every way but not crushed; we are perplexed but not in despair; we are persecuted but not abandoned; we are struck down but not destroyed.
   2 Corinthians 4:7–9

He brought me up from a desolate pit,
out of the muddy clay,
and set my feet on a rock,
making my steps secure.
He put a new song in my mouth,
a hymn of praise to our God.
Many will see and fear,
and they will trust in the LORD.
   Psalm 40:2–3

And not only that, but we also rejoice in our afflictions, because we know that affliction produces endurance, endurance produces proven character, and proven character produces hope.
    Romans 5:3–4

A person's steps are established by the LORD, and he takes pleasure in his way. Though he falls, he will not be overwhelmed, because the LORD supports him with his hand.
    Psalm 37:23–24

Brothers and sisters, I do not consider myself to have taken hold of it. But one thing I do: Forgetting what is behind and reaching forward to what is ahead, I pursue as my goal the prize promised by God's heavenly call in Christ Jesus.
    Philippians 3:13–14

Heavenly Father, thank You for your grace in times of failure, and help me press forward as I fix my eyes on Jesus.

FAITHFULNESS

God's everlasting faithfulness to His people is a deep source of hope, as well as an inspiration for how we should engage with others in our own lives.

*Because of the L*ORD*'s faithful love we do not perish, for his mercies never end. They are new every morning; great is your faithfulness!*
    Lamentations 3:22–23

His master said to him, "Well done, good and faithful servant! You were faithful over a few things; I will put you in charge of many things. Share your master's joy."
    Matthew 25:21

If we are faithless, he remains faithful, for he cannot deny himself.
    2 Timothy 2:13

Whoever is faithful in very little is also faithful in much, and whoever is unrighteous in very little is also unrighteous in much. So if you have not been faithful with worldly wealth, who will trust you with what is genuine? And if you have not been faithful with what belongs to someone else, who will give you what is your own?

Luke 16:10–12

Let us hold on to the confession of our hope without wavering, since he who promised is faithful.

Hebrews 10:23

Dear God, thank You that Your mercies are new every morning! Grant me wisdom to be faithful to my friends, my family, my employers, and my community.

FAMILY

As a recent graduate, you may be in between life with your parents and life with a spouse and children, but you can continue to practice love and faithfulness in all of your relationships.

This is why a man leaves his father and mother and bonds with his wife, and they become one flesh.
   Genesis 2:24

"Honor your father and your mother so that you may have a long life in the land that the LORD your God is giving you."
   Exodus 20:12

Fathers, don't stir up anger in your children, but bring them up in the training and instruction of the Lord.
   Ephesians 6:4

Sons are indeed a heritage from the LORD, offspring, a reward. Like arrows in the hand of a warrior are the sons born in one's youth. Happy is the man who has filled his quiver with them. They will never be put to shame when they speak with their enemies at the city gate.

Psalm 127:3–5

Wives, submit to your husbands as to the Lord, because the husband is the head of the wife as Christ is the head of the church. He is the Savior of the body. Now as the church submits to Christ, so also wives are to submit to their husbands in everything. Husbands, love your wives, just as Christ loved the church and gave himself for her to make her holy, cleansing her with the washing of water by the word. He did this to present the church to himself in splendor, without spot or wrinkle or anything like that, but holy and blameless. In the same way, husbands are to love their wives as their own bodies. He who loves his wife loves himself.

Ephesians 5:22–28

Lord, thank You for the blessings of love and grace given through my family and loved ones. May I be a reflection of Your love to my family in return.

FEAR

Most of our anxiety, dread, and unease comes not from a sense of immediate threat but from fear of what might happen in the future—but such false fear is unfounded; we have an almighty God who loves us and cares for us continually.

Haven't I commanded you: be strong and courageous? Do not be afraid or discouraged, for the LORD your God is with you wherever you go.
Joshua 1:9

When I am afraid, I will trust in you.
Psalm 56:3

You did not receive a spirit of slavery to fall back into fear. Instead, you received the Spirit of adoption, by whom we cry out, "Abba, Father!"
Romans 8:15

For God has not given us a spirit of fear, but one of power, love, and sound judgment.
    2 Timothy 1:7

⁓

Humble yourselves, therefore, under the mighty hand of God, so that he may exalt you at the proper time, casting all your cares on him, because he cares about you.
    1 Peter 5:6–7

⁓

Abba, Father, I cry out to You for Your protection and comfort in times when I'm afraid. Thank You for Your faithful love and comfort.

FORGIVENESS

Forgiving someone who has wronged you means you no longer call to mind their fault or error—this extends grace to them and freedom for you.

꧁

"Therefore I tell you, her many sins have been forgiven; that's why she loved much. But the one who is forgiven little, loves little."
   Luke 7:47

꧁

Live in harmony with one another. Do not be proud; instead, associate with the humble. Do not be wise in your own estimation. Do not repay anyone evil for evil. Give careful thought to do what is honorable in everyone's eyes. If possible, as far as it depends on you, live at peace with everyone.
   Romans 12:16–18

Be kind and compassionate to one another, forgiving one another, just as God also forgave you in Christ.
    Ephesians 4:32

෴

As God's chosen ones, holy and dearly loved, put on compassion, kindness, humility, gentleness, and patience, bearing with one another and forgiving one another if anyone has a grievance against another. Just as the Lord has forgiven you, so you are also to forgive.
    Colossians 3:12–13

෴

Lord God, just as You forgave all my debts and wrongs through Christ, empower me to extend forgiveness to anyone who has hurt me.

FRIENDSHIP

True friendship goes beyond text messages and social media posts, and a godly friend will build you up and encourage you in your walk with Christ.

∽

Two are better than one because they have a good reward for their efforts. For if either falls, his companion can lift him up; but pity the one who falls without another to lift him up.
   Ecclesiastes 4:9–10

∽

No one has greater love than this: to lay down his life for his friends. You are my friends if you do what I command you. I do not call you servants anymore, because a servant doesn't know what his master is doing. I have called you friends, because I have made known to you everything I have heard from my Father.
   John 15:13–15

Iron sharpens iron,
and one person sharpens another.
    Proverbs 27:17

₿

Dear friends, let us love one another, because love is from God, and
everyone who loves has been born of God and knows God.
    1 John 4:7

₿

Therefore encourage one another and build each other up as you are
already doing.
    1 Thessalonians 5:11

₿

Lord Jesus, who called His disciples friends,
thank You for demonstrating God's love
for us and how best to love one another.

FUTURE

God's grace and His purposes have assured your future, which grants you the freedom to live fully, faithfully, and fearlessly in the present moment.

∽

The LORD will fulfill his purpose for me.
LORD, your faithful love endures forever;
do not abandon the work of your hands.
    Psalm 138:8

∽

A person's heart plans his way,
but the Lord determines his steps.
    Proverbs 16:9

∽

"For I know the plans I have for you"—this is the LORD's declaration—
"plans for your well-being, not for disaster, to give you a future and a hope."
    Jeremiah 29:11

But our citizenship is in heaven, and we eagerly wait for a Savior from there, the Lord Jesus Christ. He will transform the body of our humble condition into the likeness of his glorious body, by the power that enables him to subject everything to himself.

Philippians 3:20–21

Dear friends, we are God's children now, and what we will be has not yet been revealed. We know that when he appears, we will be like him because we will see him as he is.

1 John 3:2

Dear Lord, help me remember that my past, present, and future are all in Your hands.

GENEROSITY

Generosity is about much more than giving away money—it's also about freely giving of your time, energy, and resources, knowing that all good things have been entrusted to you from the Lord.

Good will come to the one who lends generously
and conducts his business fairly.
   Psalm 112:5

And if you lend to those from whom you expect to receive, what credit
is that to you? Even sinners lend to sinners to be repaid in full. But love
your enemies, do what is good, and lend, expecting nothing in return.
Then your reward will be great, and you will be children of the Most
High. For he is gracious to the ungrateful and evil.
   Luke 6:34–35

Give, and it will be given to you; a good measure—pressed down, shaken together, and running over—will be poured into your lap. For with the measure you use, it will be measured back to you.
   Luke 6:38

∽

No one is to seek his own good, but the good of the other person.
   1 Corinthians 10:24

∽

Each person should do as he has decided in his heart—not reluctantly or out of compulsion, since God loves a cheerful giver.
   2 Corinthians 9:7

∽

Heavenly Father, who gives generously from his riches of grace in Christ Jesus, help me give freely from Your abundant blessings.

GRACE

The greatest gift we will ever receive is grace—the wholly unmerited favor of the Most High.

The law came along to multiply the trespass. But where sin multiplied, grace multiplied even more.
    Romans 5:20

For sin will not rule over you, because you are not under the law but under grace.
    Romans 6:14

Now if by grace, then it is not by works; otherwise grace ceases to be grace.
    Romans 11:6

But he said to me, "My grace is sufficient for you, for my power is perfected in weakness."
Therefore, I will most gladly boast all the more about my weaknesses, so that Christ's power may reside in me.
   2 Corinthians 12:9

∽

For you are saved by grace through faith, and this is not from yourselves; it is God's gift—not from works, so that no one can boast.
   Ephesians 2:8–9

∽

Lord God, thank You for Your riches of grace that have been poured out on me through faith in Christ Jesus.

GRIEF

The deep sorrow of grief that comes from losing a loved one, a pet, or even a job can seem profound and unending—but God promises to be near us, to comfort us, and to bring joy and beauty out of the ashes.

The righteous cry out, and the LORD hears,
and rescues them from all their troubles.
The LORD is near the brokenhearted;
he saves those crushed in spirit.
    Psalm 34:17–18

Why, my soul, are you so dejected?
Why are you in such turmoil?
Put your hope in God, for I will still praise him,
my Savior and my God.
    Psalm 42:5

Then the young women will rejoice with dancing, while young and old men rejoice together. I will turn their mourning into joy, give them consolation, and bring happiness out of grief.
    Jeremiah 31:13

Though the fig tree does not bud and there is no fruit on the vines, though the olive crop fails and the fields produce no food, though the flocks disappear from the pen and there are no herds in the stalls, yet I will celebrate in the Lord; I will rejoice in the God of my salvation!
    Habakkuk 3:17–18

"So you also have sorrow now. But I will see you again. Your hearts will rejoice, and no one will take away your joy from you."
    John 16:22

Heavenly Father, when my heart is aching and all I see is darkness, I trust that You are my light and my salvation.

GUILT

If we harm others or ourselves through willful or unintentional sin, guilt does not have to consume us because we know there is no condemnation for those in Christ Jesus.

As far as the east is from the west,
so far has he removed
our transgressions from us.
    Psalm 103:12

"Come, let us settle this," says the LORD. "Though your sins are scarlet, they will be as white as snow; though they are crimson red, they will be like wool."
    Isaiah 1:18

*Therefore, there is now no condemnation for those in Christ Jesus,
because the law of the Spirit of life in Christ Jesus has set you free from
the law of sin and death.*
        Romans 8:1–2

⚬

*In him we have redemption through his blood, the forgiveness of our
trespasses, according to the riches of his grace.*
        Ephesians 1:7

⚬

*If we confess our sins, he is faithful and righteous to forgive us our sins
and to cleanse us from all unrighteousness.*
        1 John 1:9

⚬

*Lord, when I have fallen short of Your glory,
grant me the wisdom to confess my sins
and be cleansed of all unrighteousness.*

HAPPINESS

Though happiness sometimes comes from external circumstances, we experience the most lasting happiness by enjoying our union with Christ.

✍

Therefore my heart is glad
and my whole being rejoices;
my body also rests securely.
        Psalm 16:9

✍

Take delight in the LORD,
and he will give you your heart's desires.
        Psalm 37:4

✍

A joyful heart makes a face cheerful,
but a sad heart produces a broken spirit.
        Proverbs 15:13

I know that there is nothing better for them than to rejoice and enjoy the good life.

    Ecclesiastes 3:12

∽

Rejoice in the Lord always. I will say it again: Rejoice!

    Philippians 4:4

∽

*Dear Jesus, may my heart be happy
and cheerful because I know You.*

HONOR

In a culture that tends to be informal and irreverent, believers can stand apart by showing honor and respect to everyone they encounter—no matter their status or station.

Honor the LḭRD with your possessions
and with the first produce of your entire harvest;
then your barns will be completely filled,
and your vats will overflow with new wine.
     Proverbs 3:9–10

Now to the King eternal, immortal, invisible, the only God, be honor
and glory forever and ever. Amen.
     1 Timothy 1:17

Pray for us, for we are convinced that we have a clear conscience, wanting to conduct ourselves honorably in everything.
Hebrews 13:18

Honor everyone. Love the brothers and sisters. Fear God. Honor the emperor.
1 Peter 2:17

Lord God, may Your Spirit guide me to honor You with my speech, actions, time, and resources.

HOPE

It's easy to put our hope in the wrong places—career, finances, social status, special relationships—but our firmest hope is found only in Christ the Redeemer.

❧

But those who trust in the LORD will renew their strength; they will soar on wings like eagles; they will run and not become weary, they will walk and not faint.
    Isaiah 40:31

❧

I wait for the LORD; I wait and put my hope in his word.
    Psalm 130:5

❧

Now may the God of hope fill you with all joy and peace as you believe so that you may overflow with hope by the power of the Holy Spirit.
    Romans 15:13

We have also obtained access through him by faith into this grace in which we stand, and we rejoice in the hope of the glory of God. And not only that, but we also rejoice in our afflictions, because we know that affliction produces endurance, endurance produces proven character, and proven character produces hope.

Romans 5:2–4

Let us run with endurance the race that lies before us, keeping our eyes on Jesus, the source and perfecter of our faith. For the joy that lay before him, he endured the cross, despising the shame, and sat down at the right hand of the throne of God.
For consider him who endured such hostility from sinners against himself, so that you won't grow weary and give up.

Hebrews 12:1–3

Lord of hope, please fill me with all joy
and peace as I wait for You.

HUMILITY

The key to cultivating true humility isn't to act self-deprecating but to simply not think of oneself much at all.

❧

Sitting down, he called the Twelve and said to them, "If anyone wants to be first, he must be last and servant of all."
   Mark 9:35

❧

"Live in harmony with one another. Do not be proud; instead, associate with the humble. Do not be wise in your own estimation."
   Romans 12:16

❧

Do nothing out of selfish ambition or conceit, but in humility consider others as more important than yourselves.
   Philippians 2:3

Adopt the same attitude as that of Christ Jesus, who, existing in the form of God, did not consider equality with God as something to be exploited. Instead he emptied himself by assuming the form of a servant, taking on the likeness of humanity. And when he had come as a man, he humbled himself by becoming obedient to the point of death—even to death on a cross.

    Philippians 2:5–8

∽

Who among you is wise and understanding? By his good conduct he should show that his works are done in the gentleness that comes from wisdom.

    James 3:13

∽

Lord Jesus, who demonstrated selflessness throughout Your earthly life, please fill my mind with thoughts of You and of others so that I forget myself completely.

IMPULSIVENESS

The feeling that most reliably follows an impulsive word or action is regret.

Discretion will watch over you,
and understanding will guard you.
It will rescue you from the way of evil—
from anyone who says perverse things,
      Proverbs 2:11–12

So if you have been raised with Christ, seek the things above, where Christ is, seated at the right hand of God. Set your minds on things above, not on earthly things.
      Colossians 3:1–2

For we all stumble in many ways. If anyone does not stumble in what he says, he is mature, able also to control the whole body.

James 3:2

Watch yourselves so you don't lose what we have worked for, but that you may receive a full reward. Anyone who does not remain in Christ's teaching but goes beyond it does not have God. The one who remains in that teaching, this one has both the Father and the Son.

2 John 8–9

Lord God, I am confident that I will see Your goodness in the land of the living; may Your Spirit empower me to be strong and wait for You.

INTEGRITY

The late basketball coach John Wooden once said, "The true test of a person's character is what he does when no one is watching."

The one who lives with integrity lives securely,
but whoever perverts his ways will be found out.
    Proverbs 10:9

Better the poor person who lives with integrity
than the rich one who distorts right and wrong.
    Proverbs 28:6

Indeed, we are giving careful thought to do what is right, not only before
the Lord but also before people.
    2 Corinthians 8:21

Whatever you do, do it from the heart, as something done for the Lord and not for people, knowing that you will receive the reward of an inheritance from the Lord. You serve the Lord Christ.
   Colossians 3:23–24

∽

Yet do this with gentleness and respect, keeping a clear conscience, so that when you are accused, those who disparage your good conduct in Christ will be put to shame.
   1 Peter 3:16

∽

Search me, God, and know my heart,
and if there is anything offensive in me,
lead me in the way everlasting.

JOY

Happiness can be fleeting, but joy is steadfast because it is a state of being rooted in our soul's intimacy with Christ.

᠅

You reveal the path of life to me;
in your presence is abundant joy;
at your right hand are eternal pleasures.
   Psalm 16:11

᠅

This is the day the Lord has made;
let us rejoice and be glad in it.
   Psalm 118:24

But the fruit of the Spirit is love, joy, peace, patience, kindness, goodness, faithfulness, gentleness, and self-control. The law is not against such things.
    Galatians 5:22–23

"As the Father has loved me, I have also loved you. Remain in my love. If you keep my commands you will remain in my love, just as I have kept my Father's commands and remain in his love.
"I have told you these things so that my joy may be in you and your joy may be complete."
    John 15:9–11

Heavenly Father, thank You for Your faithfulness,
for in Your presence is abundant joy.

KNOWLEDGE

Though you may have spent years studying school books, the truest knowledge is the awe and reverence of the Creator.

❧

For wisdom will enter your heart,
and knowledge will delight you.
> *Proverbs 2:10*

❧

The mind of the discerning acquires knowledge,
and the ear of the wise seeks it.
> *Proverbs 18:15*

❧

For the earth will be filled with the knowledge of the Lord's glory, as the
water covers the sea.
> *Habakkuk 2:14*

We know that "we all have knowledge." Knowledge puffs up, but love builds up. If anyone thinks he knows anything, he does not yet know it as he ought to know it. But if anyone loves God, he is known by him.

    1 Corinthians 8:1–3

↝

For this reason also, since the day we heard this, we haven't stopped praying for you. We are asking that you may be filled with the knowledge of his will in all wisdom and spiritual understanding, so that you may walk worthy of the Lord, fully pleasing to him: bearing fruit in every good work and growing in the knowledge of God, being strengthened with all power, according to his glorious might, so that you may have great endurance and patience, joyfully giving thanks to the Father, who has enabled you to share in the saints' inheritance in the light.

    Colossians 1:9–12

↝

Dear God, please fill me with Your Holy Spirit to teach me Your Word and guide me in Your ways.

LAZINESS

Work of all kinds is a gift from God to provide us with not only a living but also a sense of purpose and service to others.

❧

The slacker craves, yet has nothing,
but the diligent is fully satisfied.
Proverbs 13:4

❧

The one who is lazy in his work
is brother to a vandal.
Proverbs 18:9

Whatever you do, do it from the heart, as something done for the Lord and not for people, knowing that you will receive the reward of an inheritance from the Lord. You serve the Lord Christ.
    Colossians 3:23–24

∽

In fact, when we were with you, this is what we commanded you: "If anyone isn't willing to work, he should not eat."
    2 Thessalonians 3:10

∽

Lord, when I'm feeling weary and tired, please strengthen me with the power of Your Holy Spirit.

LEADERSHIP

A true leader isn't one who has climbed to the top of a hierarchy, but one who chooses above all else to be a servant to all.

Jesus called them over and said, "You know that the rulers of the Gentiles lord it over them, and those in high positions act as tyrants over them. It must not be like that among you. On the contrary, whoever wants to become great among you must be your servant, and whoever wants to be first among you must be your slave; just as the Son of Man did not come to be served, but to serve, and to give his life as a ransom for many."
    Matthew 20:25–28

Don't let anyone despise your youth, but set an example for the believers in speech, in conduct, in love, in faith, and in purity.
    1 Timothy 4:12

Adopt the same attitude as that of Christ Jesus, who, existing in the form of God, did not consider equality with God as something to be exploited. Instead he emptied himself by assuming the form of a servant, taking on the likeness of humanity. And when he had come as a man, he humbled himself by becoming obedient to the point of death—even to death on a cross. For this reason God highly exalted him and gave him the name that is above every name, so that at the name of Jesus every knee will bow—in heaven and on earth and under the earth—and every tongue will confess that Jesus Christ is Lord, to the glory of God the Father.

    Philippians 2:5–11

Shepherd God's flock among you, not overseeing out of compulsion but willingly, as God would have you; not out of greed for money but eagerly; not lording it over those entrusted to you, but being examples to the flock. And when the chief Shepherd appears, you will receive the unfading crown of glory.

    1 Peter 5:2–4

Lord Jesus, You came not to be served but to serve; grant me Your Spirit of servant leadership in my endeavors.

LONELINESS

Despite our constant online connections, many of us often feel isolated and lonely—but thanks to God's faithful presence and our community of believers, we are never truly alone.

"My presence will go with you, and I will give you rest."
Exodus 33:14

The LORD is the one who will go before you. He will be with you; he will not leave you or abandon you. Do not be afraid or discouraged.
Deuteronomy 31:8

God provides homes for those who are deserted.
He leads out the prisoners to prosperity,
but the rebellious live in a scorched land.
Psalm 68:6

He heals the brokenhearted
and bandages their wounds.
Psalm 147:3

∽

Blessed be the God and Father of our Lord Jesus Christ, the Father of
mercies and the God of all comfort. He comforts us in all our affliction,
so that we may be able to comfort those who are in any kind of affliction,
through the comfort we ourselves receive from God.
2 Corinthians 1:3–4

∽

Father of mercies, please comfort me in times of
loneliness so I may be a comfort to others.

LOVE

Our highest calling is to love God with all of our heart, our soul, and our mind, and to love our neighbor as ourselves.

"But I say to you who listen: Love your enemies, do what is good to those who hate you, bless those who curse you, pray for those who mistreat you."

　　Luke 6:27–28

Love is patient, love is kind. Love does not envy, is not boastful, is not arrogant, is not rude, is not self-seeking, is not irritable, and does not keep a record of wrongs.

　　1 Corinthians 13:4–5

Above all, maintain constant love for one another, since love covers a multitude of sins.
    1 Peter 4:8

✍

God's love was revealed among us in this way: God sent his one and only Son into the world so that we might live through him.
    1 John 4:9

✍

And we have come to know and to believe the love that God has for us. God is love, and the one who remains in love remains in God, and God remains in him.
    1 John 4:16

✍

Dear Jesus, instill in my heart the kind of selfless concern for the well-being of others that You demonstrated for us.

MOTIVES

Rather than self-seeking or people-pleasing, let everything you do come from genuine love for God and others.

෴

But the LORD said to Samuel, "Do not look at his appearance or his stature because I have rejected him. Humans do not see what the LORD sees, for humans see what is visible, but the LORD sees the heart."
  1 Samuel 16:7

෴

All a person's ways seem right to him,
but the LORD weighs hearts.
  Proverbs 21:2

෴

For am I now trying to persuade people, or God? Or am I striving to please people? If I were still trying to please people, I would not be a servant of Christ.
  Galatians 1:10

Do nothing out of selfish ambition or conceit, but in humility consider others as more important than yourselves.
  Philippians 2:3

✍

Instead, just as we have been approved by God to be entrusted with the gospel, so we speak, not to please people, but rather God, who examines our hearts.
  1 Thessalonians 2:4

✍

Lord God, please weigh my heart and my reasons for doing the things I do, and reveal to me any motives that don't glorify You.

OBEDIENCE

Obedience to God means yielding our will to His, and His will is that we love Him and our neighbor as ourselves—on these two commandments depend all the law and the prophets.

❧

I have chosen the way of truth;
I have set your ordinances before me.
    Psalm 119:30

❧

"If you love me, you will keep my commands."
    John 14:15

❧

Peter and the apostles replied, "We must obey God rather than people."
    Acts 5:29

The one who keeps his commands remains in him, and he in him. And the way we know that he remains in us is from the Spirit he has given us.
        1 John 3:24

∽

For this is what love for God is: to keep his commands. And his commands are not a burden, because everyone who has been born of God conquers the world. This is the victory that has conquered the world: our faith.
        1 John 5:3–4

∽

Lord Jesus, may Your Spirit guide me in all my thoughts, words, and actions that I may be fully submitted to Your will.

PATIENCE

Modern life moves fast, and we are often hard-pressed and harried—but a lack of patience can lead to wrong choices or damaged relationships.

✄

The end of a matter is better than its beginning; a patient spirit is better than a proud spirit.
    Ecclesiastes 7:8

✄

Now if we hope for what we do not see, we eagerly wait for it with patience.
    Romans 8:25

✄

My dear brothers and sisters, understand this: Everyone should be quick to listen, slow to speak, and slow to anger, for human anger does not accomplish God's righteousness.
    James 1:19–20

Therefore, brothers and sisters, be patient until the Lord's coming. See how the farmer waits for the precious fruit of the earth and is patient with it until it receives the early and the late rains. You also must be patient. Strengthen your hearts, because the Lord's coming is near.
    James 5:7–8

✍

The Lord does not delay his promise, as some understand delay, but is patient with you, not wanting any to perish but all to come to repentance.
    2 Peter 3:9

✍

Heavenly Father, You are patient and slow to anger; please help me be still and wait patiently for You.

PEACE

The way to peace is to quiet the ruminating mind, which worries over what has happened in the past and what might happen in the future.

You will keep the mind that is dependent on you in perfect peace, for it is trusting in you.
    Isaiah 26:3

"Peace I leave with you. My peace I give to you. I do not give to you as the world gives. Don't let your heart be troubled or fearful."
    John 14:27

For I am persuaded that neither death nor life, nor angels nor rulers, nor things present nor things to come, nor powers, nor height nor depth, nor any other created thing will be able to separate us from the love of God that is in Christ Jesus our Lord.

Romans 8:38–39

And the peace of God, which surpasses all understanding, will guard your hearts and minds in Christ Jesus. Finally brothers and sisters, whatever is true, whatever is honorable, whatever is just, whatever is pure, whatever is lovely, whatever is commendable—if there is any moral excellence and if there is anything praiseworthy—dwell on these things.

Philippians 4:7–8

Lord Jesus, may Your perfect peace guard my heart and mind as I trust in You.

PERSEVERANCE

No matter what trial you face or how exhausted you may feel, remember that the Lord upholds you and strengthens you at all times.

And not only that, but we also rejoice in our afflictions, because we know that affliction produces endurance, endurance produces proven character, and proven character produces hope. This hope will not disappoint us, because God's love has been poured out in our hearts through the Holy Spirit who was given to us.
    Romans 5:3–5

Therefore, since we also have such a large cloud of witnesses surrounding us, let us lay aside every hindrance and the sin that so easily ensnares us. Let us run with endurance the race that lies before us, keeping our eyes on Jesus, the source and perfecter of our faith. For the joy that lay before him, he endured the cross, despising the shame, and sat down at the right hand of the throne of God.
    Hebrews 12:1–2

*Let us not get tired of doing good, for we will reap at the proper time if
we don't give up.*
Galatians 6:9

∾

*Consider it a great joy, my brothers and sisters, whenever you
experience various trials, because you know that the testing of your
faith produces endurance. And let endurance have its full effect, so that
you may be mature and complete, lacking nothing.*
James 1:2–4

∾

*Blessed is the one who endures trials, because when he has stood the test
he will receive the crown of life that God has promised to those who love
him.*
James 1:12

∾

*Dear Jesus, help me fix my eyes on You that Your
Spirit may strengthen my heart and will to persevere.*

POOR

A person who earns only the median income in the United States is still richer than 99.8 percent of the world's population—our poverty can be found in a lack of gratitude for such abundance.

"Because of the devastation of the needy
and the groaning of the poor,
I will now rise up," says the LORD.
"I will provide safety for the one who longs for it."
    Psalm 12:5

Then looking up at his disciples, he said: "Blessed are you who are poor, because the kingdom of God is yours. Blessed are you who are now hungry, because you will be filled."
    Luke 6:20–21

For you know the grace of our Lord Jesus Christ: Though he was rich, for your sake he became poor, so that by his poverty you might become rich.

  2 Corinthians 8:9

✑

Listen, my dear brothers and sisters: Didn't God choose the poor in this world to be rich in faith and heirs of the kingdom that he has promised to those who love him?

  James 2:5

✑

If anyone has this world's goods and sees a fellow believer in need but withholds compassion from him—how does God's love reside in him?

  1 John 3:17

✑

Lord Jesus, You being rich became poor for our sake—may Your compassion flow through me to help those in need.

PRAYER

No matter how we come to the Lord, whether to present our requests and needs or to sit silently in His presence, we can trust that He hears us.

"Whenever you pray, you must not be like the hypocrites, because they love to pray standing in the synagogues and on the street corners to be seen by people. Truly I tell you, they have their reward. But when you pray, go into your private room, shut your door, and pray to your Father who is in secret. And your Father who sees in secret will reward you. When you pray, don't babble like the Gentiles, since they imagine they'll be heard for their many words. Don't be like them, because your Father knows the things you need before you ask him.

"Therefore, you should pray like this: Our Father in heaven, your name be honored as holy. Your kingdom come. Your will be done on earth as it is in heaven. Give us today our daily bread. And forgive us our debts, as we also have forgiven our debtors. And do not bring us into temptation, but deliver us from the evil one.

"For if you forgive others their offenses, your heavenly Father will forgive you as well. But if you don't forgive others, your Father will not forgive your offenses."

    Matthew 6:5–15

"If you remain in me and my words remain in you, ask whatever you want and it will be done for you."
   John 15:7

⚮

In the same way the Spirit also helps us in our weakness, because we do not know what to pray for as we should, but the Spirit himself intercedes for us with unspoken groanings.
   Romans 8:26

⚮

Don't worry about anything, but in everything, through prayer and petition with thanksgiving, present your requests to God.
   Philippians 4:6

⚮

Pray constantly.
   1 Thessalonians 5:17

⚮

Lord Jesus, just as You taught Your followers how to pray, instill in me a deep desire to seek Your presence.

PRIDE

Social media, while keeping us connected, has also created a culture of narcissism and egocentricity—but placing so much emphasis on oneself is neither godly nor healthy.

∽

When arrogance comes, disgrace follows,
but with humility comes wisdom.
      Proverbs 11:2

∽

Everyone with a proud heart is detestable to the LORD;
be assured, he will not go unpunished.
      Proverbs 16:5

∽

A person's pride will humble him,
but a humble spirit will gain honor.
      Proverbs 29:23

Live in harmony with one another. Do not be proud; instead, associate with the humble. Do not be wise in your own estimation.
Romans 12:16

For if anyone considers himself to be something when he is nothing, he deceives himself.
Galatians 6:3

Lord God, please forgive the ways I allow my ego to direct my thoughts and actions, and help me center my heart on You.

PURPOSE

We often seek our purpose in our vocations or careers, but our deepest purpose is not in what we do but in who we are—people who love, honor, and praise God.

⚜

When all has been heard, the conclusion of the matter is this: fear God and keep his commands, because this is for all humanity.
  Ecclesiastes 12:13

⚜

"My Father is glorified by this: that you produce much fruit and prove to be my disciples."
  John 15:8

⚜

But I consider my life of no value to myself; my purpose is to finish my course and the ministry I received from the Lord Jesus, to testify to the gospel of God's grace.
  Acts 20:24

He has saved us and called us with a holy calling, not according to our works, but according to his own purpose and grace, which was given to us in Christ Jesus before time began.
    2 Timothy 1:9

∽

Sing to him; sing praise to him; tell about all his wondrous works! Honor his holy name; let the hearts of those who seek the LORD rejoice.
    1 Chronicles 16:9–10

∽

Lord Jesus, may each day offer me opportunities to live out my true purpose by loving and serving You and those around me.

RELATIONSHIPS

Loving relationships and friendships are gifts from God—we are built up and supported in community and in fellowship with other believers.

∽

*Then the L*ORD *God said, "It is not good for the man to be alone. I will make a helper corresponding to him."*
    Genesis 2:18

∽

But if they do not have self-control, they should marry, since it is better to marry than to burn with desire.
    1 Corinthians 7:9

∽

Don't become partners with those who do not believe. For what partnership is there between righteousness and lawlessness? Or what fellowship does light have with darkness?
    2 Corinthians 6:14

Therefore encourage one another and build each other up as you are already doing.
    1 Thessalonians 5:11

❦

Above all, maintain constant love for one another, since love covers a multitude of sins.
    1 Peter 4:8

❦

Heavenly Father, reveal to me ways I can be a conduit of Your love toward those in my community today.

RELIABILITY

In modern society, some people think little of "flaking" on others, but believers can stand apart by being dependable and committed to our word.

❧

He will not allow your foot to slip;
your Protector will not slumber.
> *Psalm 121:3*

❧

"But let your 'yes' mean 'yes,' and your 'no' mean 'no.' Anything more
than this is from the evil one."
> *Matthew 5:37*

"Whoever is faithful in very little is also faithful in much, and whoever is unrighteous in very little is also unrighteous in much."
    Luke 16:10

∽

What you have heard from me in the presence of many witnesses, commit to faithful men who will be able to teach others also.
    2 Timothy 2:2

∽

Lord, just as you are constant and faithful, help me to be someone others can reliably depend upon.

SAVIOR

Our Savior is Jesus, the Source and Perfector of our faith, who for the joy set before Him endured the cross.

He said, "They are indeed my people, children who will not be disloyal," and he became their Savior. In all their suffering, he suffered, and the angel of his presence saved them. He redeemed them because of his love and compassion; he lifted them up and carried them all the days of the past.

Isaiah 63:8–9

My soul praises the greatness of the Lord, and my spirit rejoices in God my Savior, because he has looked with favor on the humble condition of his servant.

Luke 1:46–48

This Jesus is the stone rejected by you builders, which has become the cornerstone. There is salvation in no one else, for there is no other name under heaven given to people by which we must be saved.

Acts 4:11–12

This is good, and it pleases God our Savior, who wants everyone to be saved and to come to the knowledge of the truth.

1 Timothy 2:3–4

And we have seen and we testify that the Father has sent his Son as the world's Savior.

1 John 4:14

*Lord Jesus, I have been crucified with You—
may the life I now live be lived for You who
loved me and gave Yourself for me.*

SELF-CONTROL

We often think about self-control in terms of moral behavior, but consider also the importance of holding our tongues—especially when reacting to social media.

❧

A person who does not control his temper
is like a city whose wall is broken down.
  Proverbs 25:28

❧

No temptation has come upon you except what is common to humanity.
But God is faithful; he will not allow you to be tempted beyond what you
are able, but with the temptation he will also provide a way out so that
you may be able to bear it.
  1 Corinthians 10:13

Finally brothers and sisters, whatever is true, whatever is honorable, whatever is just, whatever is pure, whatever is lovely, whatever is commendable—if there is any moral excellence and if there is anything praiseworthy—dwell on these things.

Philippians 4:8

෧෧

Be sober-minded, be alert. Your adversary the devil is prowling around like a roaring lion, looking for anyone he can devour.

1 Peter 5:8

෧෧

Lord God, when I struggle with temptation or am quick to anger, please renew Your Spirit within me.

SERVICE

If Jesus, the King of Heaven, came not to be served but to serve others, how can we do any less?

"And the King will answer them, 'Truly I tell you, whatever you did for one of the least of these brothers and sisters of mine, you did for me.'"
    Matthew 25:40

"For even the Son of Man did not come to be served, but to serve, and to give his life as a ransom for many."
    Mark 10:45

I have been crucified with Christ, and I no longer live, but Christ lives in me. The life I now live in the body, I live by faith in the Son of God, who loved me and gave himself for me.
    Galatians 2:20

Therefore, my dear brothers and sisters, be steadfast, immovable, always excelling in the Lord's work, because you know that your labor in the Lord is not in vain.

1 Corinthians 15:58

Lord Jesus, please open my eyes to see the myriad opportunities to serve others, and open my heart to do so freely and with compassion.

SPEECH

When we speak, the words we choose are only part of our response—we must also consider our motives and tone of voice.

❧

A gentle answer turns away anger,
but a harsh word stirs up wrath.
Proverbs 15:1

❧

Let your speech always be gracious, seasoned with salt, so that you may know how you should answer each person.
Colossians 4:6

❧

Bless those who persecute you; bless and do not curse.
Romans 12:14

But no one can tame the tongue. It is a restless evil, full of deadly poison. With the tongue we bless our Lord and Father, and with it we curse people who are made in God's likeness. Blessing and cursing come out of the same mouth. My brothers and sisters, these things should not be this way.

James 3:8–10

§

No foul language should come from your mouth, but only what is good for building up someone in need, so that it gives grace to those who hear.

Ephesians 4:29

§

Holy Spirit, please fill my heart with the gracious love of God so that my speech is humble, gentle, and kind.

STABILITY

Little in life ever stays the same, but even when our circumstances are shifting, we have a firm foundation in Christ Jesus.

∽

I always let the LORD guide me.
Because he is at my right hand,
I will not be shaken.
        Psalm 16:8

∽

He brought me up from a desolate pit,
out of the muddy clay,
and set my feet on a rock,
making my steps secure.
        Psalm 40:2

The person who trusts in the LORD, whose confidence indeed is the LORD, is blessed. He will be like a tree planted by water: it sends its roots out toward a stream, it doesn't fear when heat comes, and its foliage remains green. It will not worry in a year of drought or cease producing fruit.

Jeremiah 17:7–8

Therefore, since we are receiving a kingdom that cannot be shaken, let us be thankful. By it, we may serve God acceptably, with reverence and awe, for our God is a consuming fire.

Hebrews 12:28–29

Dear God, there is no one besides You, nor do I have any rock like You.

STRESS

Chronic stress is quickly becoming a national crisis that threatens our health and well-being—but God has reassured us that He is our ever-present helper in times of trouble.

✍

Cast your burden on the LORD,
and he will sustain you;
he will never allow the righteous to be shaken.
Psalm 55:22

✍

Commit your activities to the LORD,
and your plans will be established.
Proverbs 16:3

For I am the LORD your God,
who holds your right hand,
who says to you, "Do not fear,
I will help you."
      Isaiah 41:13

"Come to me, all of you who are weary and burdened, and I will give
you rest. Take up my yoke and learn from me, because I am lowly and
humble in heart, and you will find rest for your souls. For my yoke is
easy and my burden is light."
      Matthew 11:28–30

I am able to do all things through him who strengthens me.
      Philippians 4:13

Dear God, please fill me and strengthen
me with your Spirit when I feel overwhelmed,
exhausted, and uncertain.

SUCCESS

Whether you succeed or fail at your endeavors, your true identity is your relationship with the Lord Jesus.

∽

Take delight in the LORD,
and he will give you your heart's desires.
   Psalm 37:4

∽

Commit your activities to the LORD,
and your plans will be established.
   Proverbs 16:3

For what will it benefit someone if he gains the whole world yet loses his life? Or what will anyone give in exchange for his life? For the Son of Man is going to come with his angels in the glory of his Father, and then he will reward each according to what he has done.
　　Matthew 16:26–27

Humble yourselves before the Lord, and he will exalt you.
　　James 4:10

*Lord Jesus, no matter how well I do in life,
help me remember that my purpose is to be
a shining beacon of Your light and love.*

TEMPTATION

No temptation that you may face is ever unavoidable—
God is faithful to provide an escape from what tempts
you.

"Stay awake and pray, so that you won't enter into temptation. The
spirit is willing, but the flesh is weak."
    Matthew 26:41

No temptation has come upon you except what is common to humanity.
But God is faithful; he will not allow you to be tempted beyond what you
are able, but with the temptation he will also provide a way out so that
you may be able to bear it.
    1 Corinthians 10:13

For since he himself has suffered when he was tempted, he is able to help those who are tempted.

Hebrews 2:18

✍

No one undergoing a trial should say, "I am being tempted by God," since God is not tempted by evil, and he himself doesn't tempt anyone. But each person is tempted when he is drawn away and enticed by his own evil desire. Then after desire has conceived, it gives birth to sin, and when sin is fully grown, it gives birth to death.

James 1:13–15

✍

Therefore, submit to God. Resist the devil, and he will flee from you.

James 4:7

✍

Lord God, my spirit is willing, but my flesh is weak— please help me to honor You in all of my choices.

THANKFULNESS

The more we practice gratitude and thanksgiving, the more abundance and goodness we recognize all around us.

∽

Give thanks to the LORD, for he is good;
his faithful love endures forever.
    Psalm 118:1

∽

For we know that the one who raised the Lord Jesus will also raise us
with Jesus and present us with you. Indeed, everything is for your benefit
so that, as grace extends through more and more people, it may cause
thanksgiving to increase to the glory of God.
    2 Corinthians 4:14–15

Let the word of Christ dwell richly among you, in all wisdom teaching and admonishing one another through psalms, hymns, and spiritual songs, singing to God with gratitude in your hearts.
    Colossians 3:16

Rejoice always, pray constantly, give thanks in everything; for this is God's will for you in Christ Jesus.
    1 Thessalonians 5:16–18

Every good and perfect gift is from above, coming down from the Father of lights, who does not change like shifting shadows.
    James 1:17

Father of lights, I praise You and thank You for every good and perfect gift You have given.

THEFT

There are many things one might be tempted to steal—money, office supplies, ideas, recognition—but stealing reveals a heart that lacks trust in God's provision.

❧

"Do not steal."
Exodus 20:15

❧

Ill-gotten gains do not profit anyone,
but righteousness rescues from death.
Proverbs 10:2

❧

The commandments, Do not commit adultery; do not murder; do not steal; do not covet; and any other commandment, are summed up by this commandment: Love your neighbor as yourself.
Romans 13:9

Let the thief no longer steal. Instead, he is to do honest work with his own hands, so that he has something to share with anyone in need.

Ephesians 4:28

For the love of money is a root of all kinds of evil, and by craving it, some have wandered away from the faith and pierced themselves with many griefs.

1 Timothy 6:10

*Lord God, please forgive me for any instance
in which I have taken what belongs to someone
else. Please cleanse my heart of any mistrust
in Your goodness and sufficiency.*

TRUST

To trust the Lord is to believe what He has said about Himself: He is good, faithful, and sovereign.

The person who trusts in the LORD, whose confidence indeed is the LORD, is blessed. He will be like a tree planted by water: it sends its roots out toward a stream, it doesn't fear when heat comes, and its foliage remains green. It will not worry in a year of drought or cease producing fruit.

     Jeremiah 17:7–8

Wait for the LORD;
be strong, and let your heart be courageous.
Wait for the LORD.

     Psalm 27:14

"I will be with you when you pass through the waters, and when you pass through the rivers, they will not overwhelm you. You will not be scorched when you walk through the fire, and the flame will not burn you."

Isaiah 43:2

And my God will supply all your needs according to his riches in glory in Christ Jesus.

Philippians 4:19

This is the confidence we have before him: If we ask anything according to his will, he hears us.

1 John 5:14

Dear God, thank You that all things work together for the good of those who love You and are called according to Your purpose.

VIOLENCE

Whether brute force or abusive language, Jesus stood against all forms of violence and oppression, submitting even to death on a cross.

The LORD examines the righteous,
but he hates the wicked
and those who love violence.
    Psalm 11:5

Don't envy a violent man or choose any of his ways.
    Proverbs 3:31

"You have heard that it was said, An eye for an eye and a tooth for a tooth. But I tell you, don't resist an evildoer. On the contrary, if anyone slaps you on your right cheek, turn the other to him also."
     Matthew 5:38–39

Then Jesus told him, "Put your sword back in its place because all who take up the sword will perish by the sword. Or do you think that I cannot call on my Father, and he will provide me here and now with more than twelve legions of angels?"
     Matthew 26:52–53

Heavenly Father, help me realize that all the violence in the world originates in our human hearts, even mine. Cleanse us and make us people of peace.

WEALTH

God has provided richly for us with things to enjoy; therefore let us be graciousness and generous toward those in need.

ॐ

Who do I have in heaven but you?
And I desire nothing on earth but you.
    Psalm 73:25

ॐ

"Don't store up for yourselves treasures on earth, where moth and rust destroy and where thieves break in and steal. But store up for yourselves treasures in heaven, where neither moth nor rust destroys, and where thieves don't break in and steal."
    Matthew 6:19–20

I know both how to make do with little, and I know how to make do with a lot. In any and all circumstances I have learned the secret of being content—whether well fed or hungry, whether in abundance or in need.
Philippians 4:12

✧

Instruct those who are rich in the present age not to be arrogant or to set their hope on the uncertainty of wealth, but on God, who richly provides us with all things to enjoy. Instruct them to do what is good, to be rich in good works, to be generous and willing to share, storing up treasure for themselves as a good foundation for the coming age, so that they may take hold of what is truly life.
1 Timothy 6:17–19

✧

*Lord Jesus, I praise You and thank You
that my richest gain is knowing You.*

WISDOM

After graduating from school, we may have extensive knowledge, but wisdom comes from the Holy Spirit, who helps us discern what is true, good, and right.

∽

Teach us to number our days carefully
so that we may develop wisdom in our hearts.
    Psalm 90:12

∽

Do not be conformed to this age, but be transformed by the renewing
of your mind, so that you may discern what is the good, pleasing, and
perfect will of God.
    Romans 12:2

Yet to those who are called, both Jews and Greeks, Christ is the power of God and the wisdom of God, because God's foolishness is wiser than human wisdom, and God's weakness is stronger than human strength.
    1 Corinthians 1:24–25

∽

Now if any of you lacks wisdom, he should ask God—who gives to all generously and ungrudgingly—and it will be given to him.
    James 1:5

∽

Heavenly Father, who gives generously and ungrudgingly, please fill me with Your wisdom.

WORK

Our ability to work is a gift from God—we can create and produce for the good of the world around us, which glorifies the Creator.

✍

Commit your activities to the LORD,
and your plans will be established.
Proverbs 16:3

✍

Do everything in love.
1 Corinthians 16:14

✍

And God is able to make every grace overflow to you, so that in every
way, always having everything you need, you may excel in every good
work.
2 Corinthians 9:8

Whatever you do, do it from the heart, as something done for the Lord and not for people, knowing that you will receive the reward of an inheritance from the Lord. You serve the Lord Christ.

Colossians 3:23–24

Come now, you who say, "Today or tomorrow we will travel to such and such a city and spend a year there and do business and make a profit." Yet you do not know what tomorrow will bring—what your life will be! For you are like vapor that appears for a little while, then vanishes. Instead, you should say, "If the Lord wills, we will live and do this or that."

James 4:13–15

Creator of all good things, grant me meaningful work and empower me to do everything as for You and not for people.

WORRY

Worry is false and useless fear: it's imagining and anticipating what might happen but probably won't.

"Therefore I tell you: Don't worry about your life, what you will eat or what you will drink; or about your body, what you will wear. Isn't life more than food and the body more than clothing? Consider the birds of the sky: They don't sow or reap or gather into barns, yet your heavenly Father feeds them. Aren't you worth more than they? Can any of you add one moment to his life-span by worrying?"
    Matthew 6:25–27

The Lord answered her, "Martha, Martha, you are worried and upset about many things, but one thing is necessary. Mary has made the right choice, and it will not be taken away from her."
    Luke 10:41–42

We know that all things work together for the good of those who love God, who are called according to his purpose.

   Romans 8:28

⌘

Don't worry about anything, but in everything, through prayer and petition with thanksgiving, present your requests to God. And the peace of God, which surpasses all understanding, will guard your hearts and minds in Christ Jesus.

   Philippians 4:6–7

⌘

Lord Jesus, I am often worried about many things, most of them trivial in light of Your grace and goodness. Please grant me a heart like Mary, who rested at Your feet.

VERSE INDEX